SPLURT!

BY MARTIN BAXENDALE

Published by Silent but Deadly Publications,
4 Catherine's Close, Stroud, Gloucestershire

ISBN 0 9513542 3 X
Printed in Britain by Stoate & Bishop (Printers) Ltd,
Cheltenham & Gloucester

SPLURT!
What's white and glides across the floor?
Cum dancing!
SPLAT!

SHAME
?

Premature ejaculation!
SHAME

SPLURT!
Hi, gorgeous! My name's Sammy Semen. What's yours ?
Sally Spermicide... gis' a kiss, big boy!
Cracked it!

PLOP!
Oh bloody hell! I HATE having to sleep on the WET PATCH!
SQUELCH!
It's not exactly a bundle of f***ing laughs for me either!!

SNORE!
SNORE!
SPLURT!
AAAGH!!!
WASSAT?!
SPLAT!
SNORE!
Bloody wet dream!

Fancy a game of hide-and-seek?
SPLURT!
Ready or not, here I cum!

Meet my fiancé, Sally Spermicide

It'll never last!

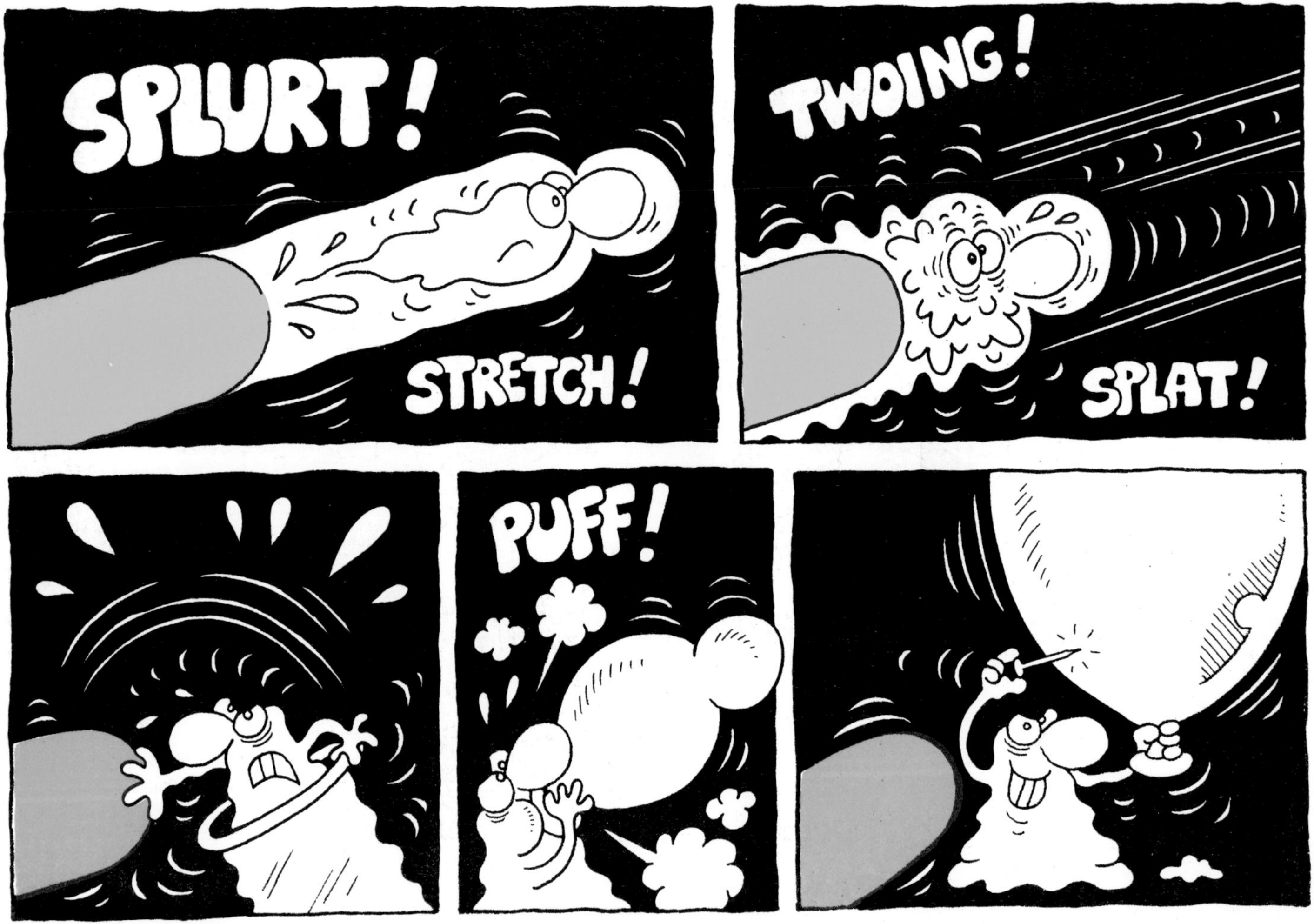
SPLURT!
STRETCH!
TWOING!
SPLAT!
PUFF!

THE PRICK IS RIGHT
Sammy Semen, CUM ON DOWN!
SPLURT!

Ooh! I've never done it out in the snow before!
BONK! BONK!

SPLURT!

Have you met my fiancé, Sally Spermicide?
THUMP!
?
Maybe you're the wrong star signs

SPLURT!
SPLAT!
Personally, I think there's a lot to be said for banning soft-porn girlie magazines!!
SPLUDGE!

SPLURT!
I must have been in every possible human orifice this week....
NOTHING could surprise me now, no matter HOW kinky....
Hello, I'm Bertie Bogie! I'd stop for a chat, but I'm just on my way out....
!

SPLURT!
GREEN-
PEACE
OZONE-FRIENDLY
CONTAINS NO CFC
GAS PROPELLANTS

Have a seat. I'll make some coffee...
Oh God! You don't actually buy these things, do you?!!
GIRLIE MAG
!
Oh! Err... Only for the feature articles and the hilarious readers' letters!

SPLURT!
PLOP!
SLIP!
?
SLIDE!

SLITHER!

SLIP!
SPLAT!

SLIDE!
Hello, I'm Vaseline Val! Who're you?

SPLURT!
?
BRRRR!
BRRRR!
BRRRR!!
BRRRR!
INFLATABLE SEX DOLL (WITH DELUXE VIBRATING NAUGHTY BITS)
BRRRR!
!

... and do you, Sally Spermicide, take Sammy Semen to be your lawfully wedded husband TILL DEATH DO YOU PART?
I do!
You may kiss the bride
SMACK!
SPLAT!
AARRGH!!
Is there a doctor in the church?

Dutch cap!

SPLURT!
SPLURT!
Amazing echo in here!
SPLURT!
SPLURT!
SPLURT!
SPLURT!
SPLURT!

Oh! Ah! Oh God! Don't stop! I'm...
BOING! BOING!
JIMMY THE HUMAN CANNONBALL
CIRCUS

SPLURT!
Ta-raa! Sammy the semen cannonball!!
DUTCH CAP

MARRIAGE GUIDANCE
Sammy Semen and Sally Spermicide?
COUNSELLOR
GLURK!
MARRIAGE GUIDANCE
I think we may have some basic incompatibility problems here...
COUNSELLOR

SPLURT!
God, I HATE these bloody early morning bonking sessions!
YAWN!
PLOP!
Dip! Dip!
This egg's a bit runny, darling!
SLURP!

SPLURT!

I bet you could grow some
lovely tomatoes in here!

Hey! Vaseline Val, long time no see!
Gis' a hug!
ZIP!
!
HUG!
SPLURP!

SPLURT!

I'm a star!
SPLAT!
VIDEO

NAUGHTY MASSAGE PARLOUR
SPLURT!
PLOP!
MASSAGE CREAM
MASSAGE CREAM
SPLURP!
MASSAGE CREAM
How about a spot of 'special relief' massage, darling?

I wonder where the guy who drew this stuff gets all his ideas?
I suppose they just come to him
THE END